FATHER BROWNE'S IRELAND

FATHER BROWNE'S
IRELAND

Remarkable Images of People and Places

E. E. O'Donnell SJ

WOLFHOUND PRESS

First published 1989 by
WOLFHOUND PRESS
68 Mountjoy Square,
Dublin 1.

Reprinted: 1989, 1990, 1994, 1996

British Library Cataloguing in Publication Data
Father Browne's Ireland: remarkable images of people and
    places.
    1. Ireland (Republic), 1949-
    I. O'Donnell, E. E.
    941.7082'3

ISBN 0-86327-200-2

Book and cover design: Jan de Fouw
Cover photographs: *Front*; Man of Aran 1938 (see page 98),
    Rathmines 1937; *Back*: Ferry-boat on Lough Erne 1932
    (see page 35), The Flahertys of Oghill, The Aran Islands
    1938. Separations: Graphic Reproductions Ltd.
Photographic prints by David H. Davison,
    Pieterse-Davison International Ltd., Dublin.
Duotone separations: Colour Repro Ltd., Dublin.
Typesetting and layout: Redsetter Ltd., Dublin.
Printed in Hong Kong through World Print Ltd., 1996.

CONTENTS

Continued overleaf

Connacht

Self-portrait at Maam, Connemara.

INTRODUCTION

Just a few weeks ago I received a letter from a man I have never met, Mr Thomas E. Eustace. It began like this:

I had the pleasure of presenting your book *The Annals of Dublin* to my father on his 78th birthday the other day. He said that he knew Fr Browne well as he often went on cycling trips with him while my father was a student in Belvedere.

My father's father was a busy G.P. who lived on Parnell Square. He had two cars, a Buick and a small Citroën and from time to time Fr Browne would borrow the Buick for one of his various expeditions. One Sunday afternoon, my grandfather was trundling up the Phoenix Park in the little Citroën when the Buick roared past nearly sweeping him off the road. That apparently ended Fr Browne's borrowings of the Buick.

These paragraphs are worth quoting because they capture the spirit of Frank Browne: a man in a hurry. He was forever darting around the country as a Jesuit priest, giving a retreat here or a parish mission there, driving to photograph a wedding in Donegal, popping down by train to photograph the interior of a noble house in County Cork. One wonders how he kept going. But it is hardly surprising to hear that he left over 42,000 indexed negatives behind him when he died at the age of eighty.

Francis Mary Hegarty Browne was born in Cork in 1880. The youngest of eight children, he took his first photographs at the age of seventeen when he was brought on a Grand Tour of Europe. In September 1897 he joined the Jesuit Order and was ordained eighteen years later (1915) by his uncle, Robert Browne, Bishop of Cloyne. This was the uncle who had bought Frank a ticket for the first stage of a famous maiden voyage, that of the *Titanic*. Frank sailed from Southampton to Queenstown (Cobh) where he disembarked with a remarkable set of photographs, including the only one ever taken in the doomed liner's radio-room. When the ship sank, Browne became famous. Many of his pictures appeared on the front page (and inside pages) of London's *Daily Sketch* and other newspapers.

That was not the only adventure in Frank Browne's early years. Before the Easter Rising of 1916, he was sent as chaplain to the Irish Guards. He served with them in France and Flanders until the end of World War I, winning the British Military Cross and the Belgian Croix de Guerre. During this time he became a personal friend of General Alexander who described Frank as the bravest man he had ever met. As Lord Alexander of Tunis, he came to visit Father Browne on his death-bed in 1960.

In the obituary notice which he wrote for the *Irish Guards Association Journal*, Lt. Col. Lord Nugent wrote:

Father Browne was a man of infinite humour and he loved a good argument. When he was excited the words poured from him and he had an engaging habit of interjecting 'Yes, Yes' into his conversation. In moments of particular excitement he was inclined to become incoherent and let his imagination run riot as when he assured an astonished and incredulous Battalion Headquarters in Bourlon Wood in 1917 that on his way from visiting wounded during that chaotic battle he had seen 'scores of Germans. Yes, Yes, pouring through the wood with their bayonets fixed on their Lewis Guns!'

Since 1919 when he left the Battalion he lived in Ireland and seldom came to England, but whenever he did he sought out his old friends whom he never forgot. A few days before he died the Colonel of the Regiment went to see him in hospital. Though barely conscious he rallied, recognised the Colonel and asked after the Regiment he loved and had served so well. A great Christian, a brave and lovable man, we who knew him will always be grateful for his friendship and the example that he set.

When he retired from the Irish Guards in 1919, Father Browne taught for three years at Belvedere College in Dublin and then became Superior of St Francis Xavier's Church, Gardiner Street, until 1928. It was during this period that he spent nearly two years in Australia (1924-25) which at that time was part of the Irish Province of the Jesuits.

From 1928 until his death Father Browne was on the Mission Staff, an appointment which brought him to every county of Ireland as well as to England, Scotland

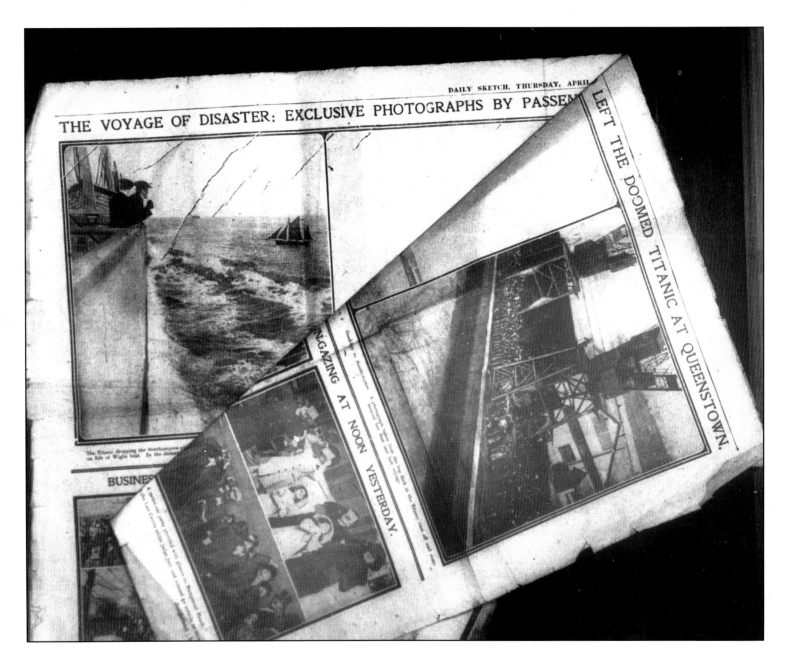

The Voyage of Disaster: Exclusive Photographs by Passengers... Left the Doomed Titanic at Queenstown. ...gazing at Noon Yesterday. Daily Sketch, Thursday, April...

and Wales. His photographic Collection includes nearly 2,000 pictures of England and over 500 of Scotland and Wales. He had taken over 800 photographs in Australia and nearly 500 on his voyages to and from that country which brought him to Spain, Italy, South Africa, Ceylon, Crete, Egypt and Aden. Back home he turned his bedroom into a veritable photographic laboratory (see illustration) where he did all his own developing.

Thus, the bulk of the Collection — a further 35,000 photographs — is Irish material. From the available negatives, one could produce books on the Great Houses of Ireland, Monastic Ireland, Railways of Ireland, Agricultural Ireland, the Electrification of Ireland, Prehistoric Ireland and so on. Such interest was shown in the Dublin photographs which illustrated their *Annals of Dublin* last year that the publishers,

Wolfhound Press, were encouraged to present more Browne photographs to the public. In this volume, it was thought best to present an overview of the Irish part of the Collection rather than to aim at any specialized readership.

This book, then, falls into four chapters representing the four provinces of Ireland. Each province has been given equal space and every county has been included.

Inevitably, this means that the provinces with more counties have fewer photographs per county, but I hope that the selection shown here will whet your appetite for future volumes.

E. E. O'Donnell, S.J.
Gonzaga College,
Dublin 6.

ULSTER

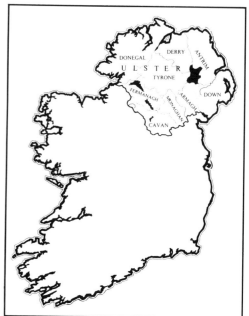

The partition of Ireland in 1922 was particularly distressing for Frank Browne. He had served in the British Army as a chaplain during World War I and had many Protestant friends north of the Border as well as south of it. He called Ireland 'Our Divided Country'; he had a special regard for Ulster, our divided province.

Three of Ulster's counties (Donegal, Monaghan and Cavan) are in the Republic of Ireland; the other six make up Northern Ireland. Father Browne's work as a priest took him to all nine counties, most often to Donegal and particularly to the Inishowen Peninsula that is tipped by Malin Head. This most northerly point in Ireland, ironically, is not in Northern Ireland. My own grandparents lived in Inishowen so I had a personal interest in seeing what the towns and the people looked like in the 1920s. In Carndonagh, for instance, I was able to discover that the Catholic church, long since translocated to the top of a nearby hill, stood just across the street from its Church of Ireland counterpart.

Donegal, of course, is the home of the ancient Clan O'Donnell. Descended from Conall, son of the famous High King of Ireland, Niall of the Nine Hostages, who reigned A.D. 379-405, the O'Donnells ruled in this part of Ireland until 1607. The Flight of the Earls (to mainland Europe from Rathmullan on Lough Swilly) in that year made way for the Plantation of Ulster and its violent consequences that have yet to run their course. The Gaelic name of the county is still *Tír Chonaill* (the land of Conall) and many of its most aged monuments – such as the Celtic Cross at Fahan – were photographed by Fr. Browne.

At the other end of the time-spectrum, we find that the most modern development was of equal interest to the photographer. He took many shots of Donegal's hydro-electric scheme near Ballyshannon. His pictures show the great dam being built on the River Erne and these make an interesting contrast with the ones he took of the construction of Poulaphuca on the Liffey and Ardnacrusha on the Shannon.

Saint Columba (an O'Donnell of royal blood) was born in Gartan in central Donegal. Before leaving Ireland for Iona and the conversion of Scotland in A.D. 563 he had already founded several monasteries in Ireland. The most notable of these was at Derry, the city whose Gaelic name is *Doire*

Edward Carson Statue, Belfast (1949).

Columcille. At the time of the Plantation, the city of London became its corporate undertaker: hence the modern prefix. 'A rose is a rose is a rose'; Londonderry is Derry is *Doire Colmcille*. The city walls that withstood a historic siege in 1689 are still intact but, curiously, Fr. Browne never photographed them. His Collection, however, provides a valuable record of the way the city used to look before the political and developmental wreckers had their respective day and say. The two cathedrals, St. Columba's (Church of Ireland) and St. Eugene's (Roman Catholic) are shown from unusual angles – a technique that was to become distinctive in Browne's work as he became more and more proficient with the camera.

County Derry used to be called Coleraine because the town of that name was bigger than Derry before the Plantation of Ulster. As a matter of cultural interest, one should note that the six counties which were 'planted' in the first decade of the seventeenth century were not the six counties that later became Northern Ireland. They were Donegal, Coleraine, Fermanagh, Tyrone, Armagh and Cavan (two of which are now in the Republic). A rich, non-Gaelic, cultural heritage is still to be found wherever the planted people took root. A recognition and an appreciation of cultural differences by 'the Olde Irishe' is still earnestly to be desired. For more on this theme I might humbly refer the reader to my book, *Northern Irish Stereotypes*, which was published by the College of Industrial Relations in 1977.

Most of County Derry is low-lying and richly agricultural. By contrast, most of Antrim is covered by a great plateau that stretches right up to the extreme north-eastern point, Torr Head, which is photographed in this chapter. The Antrim Plateau is lanced by spectacular glens. Fr. Browne was fortunate in being able to capture many of the most scenic spots while they were blanketed with snow.

In the south of the county, indeed spreading well into County Down today, Belfast lies in the shelter of Cavehill at the mouth of the River Lagan. Fr. Browne's delight in ocean-going liners would have drawn him to the great shipyards of Harland and Wolff, the pride of Belfast. (Indeed, there are plenty of maritime pictures in the Browne Collection – enough to make a book.)

Counties Antrim and Down are so close to Scotland that it comes as no surprise to learn that their history is interlinked with that country from very early times. The people of Donaghadee in County Down, for instance, used to find it a lot easier to row over to Portpatrick for their groceries or to sell their merchandise than to travel by 'road' to the nearest Irish market. These close links are still in evidence as can be seen in Fr. Browne's photography.

Moving inland to Armagh, we reach the ecclesiastical capital of Ireland, the see of St. Patrick. Both the Church of Ireland and the Church of Rome have magnificent cathedrals here and Fr. Browne shows them both together and separately. He took several portraits of Cardinals McRory and Logue over the years and he didn't fail to record the sport of road-bowling – a speciality of Counties Armagh and Cork.

Monaghan is a county that Fr. Browne visited frequently because he was a good friend of Sir Shane Leslie, cousin of Sir Winston Churchill. The fine seat of the Leslies at Glaslough was just one of many great historic residences that he photographed room by room in meticulous detail.

1579 was the date of 'the shiring of Ireland' when the present county boundaries were established. Up to then, Cavan was called 'O'Reilly's Country' (sic), a surname still prevalent there today. The county is full of lakes and, though not a fisherman himself, he was often commissioned to photograph anglers and their catches – presumably to provide proof for the doubting listener that it really was 'that big'.

Counties Fermanagh and Tyrone still have political links in terms of constituency boundaries. These links date back to the Middle Ages and beyond. The O'Neills ruled Tyrone and much of Fermanagh for generations, their holdings centering on Dungannon. Tyrone in Gaelic is Tír Eoghain (the land of Owen), named after another son of King Niall of the Nine Hostages. The County Town is now Omagh which, in Fr. Browne's day, was an important railway location. A major section of his Collection deals with trains, neatly alphabeticized under the name of the companies: G.N.R., G.S.R., L.M.S., L.N.E.R. and so on. Most of Ulster's railway lines have now closed down, so his pictorial record is particularly important.

County Fermanagh is largely comprised of two large lakes: Upper and Lower Lough Erne. It is one of the most beautiful parts of Ireland, with breath-taking scenery. Fr. Browne loved the lakes with their numerous islands and archaeological sites, and he gave several missions in the County Town of Enniskillen.

The Lawrence Collection, housed in the National Library of Ireland in Dublin, is the best-known collection of Irish photographs to date. The most notable difference between the Lawrence Collection and the Browne Collection is that Fr. Browne was interested in *people*: he wasn't just taking photographs of public buildings or scenic views for reproduction as postcards. He seemed to be more interested in capturing the spirit of a place and it would certainly appear that he found this spirit in the inhabitants. A close inspection reveals that he was fascinated by all the people of any given area – the gentry and the poor; the young and the old. In this Ulster section, as in the other three sections, I have tried to give examples of this. You will find, for example, that he photographed distinguished people like Sir Shane Leslie (see County Monaghan); 'undistinguished' people playing bowling (see County Armagh); children (see Belfast and County Tyrone); old folk (see County Down).

Just now, when writing the previous sentence, I've taken another look at the Ulster photographs and noticed that there are more photographs of children than of any other people. I ask myself, why did I include more children than adults? There is a good answer. Fr. Browne's photos of children are among his best. He seems to have been able to depict very young people more realistically than others. Grown-ups tend to be more nervous in front of a camera. More posed. Children have far fewer inhibitions. Fr. Browne was able to convey their sense of innocence in a truly remarkable way.

Overall, the Ulster photographs capture well the atmosphere of the province. In many ways Ulster has changed since the pictures were taken, but in more ways Ulster has stayed the same. In this sense there is nothing nostalgic about the images. The border post at Muff is still there. It is still 'our divided province'. Like the Titanic Memorial in Belfast, some things have changed a little. But there are still a lot of O'Neills and Carsons in Ulster.

County Donegal

Slieve League soars a sheer 1,972 feet out of Donegal Bay. During World War II, its summit was embossed with the letters EIRE as a warning to bomber pilots that they were over neutral territory. The photograph (1946) shows a wistful dreamer scanning the Atlantic for Hy Brasil.

The Free State customs post at Muff, on the road from Derry to Moville, in 1929. Kearney's Bus Service and the Inishowen Bus Service were later absorbed into the Londonderry and Lough Swilly Company.

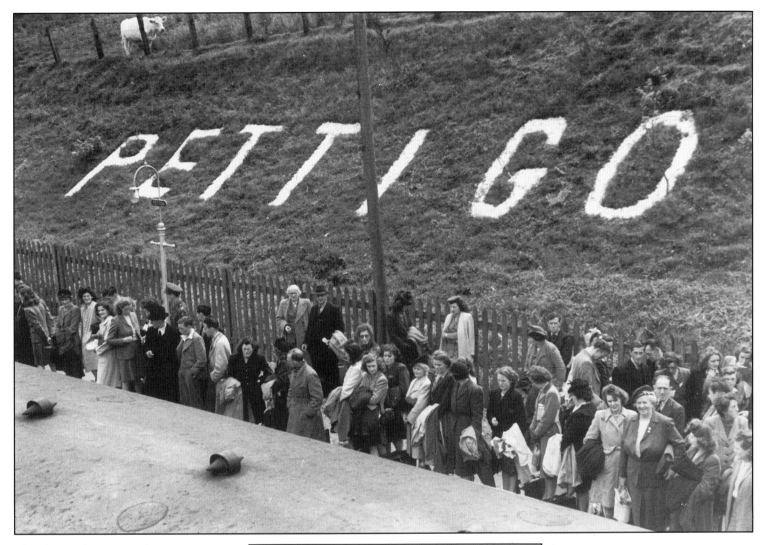

The picture shows 'starving' passengers waiting to board a train at Pettigo station in 1946. They have spent three days in penetential fasting at St. Patrick's Purgatory, Lough Derg. This railway-line was closed in 1957.

An evening view of Chapel Street, Carndonagh, 1929. This view looks southwards across the Inishowen peninsula and shows Slieve Snaght in the background. The small Catholic church on the right was replaced by a larger, hill-top edifice which now dominates the town.

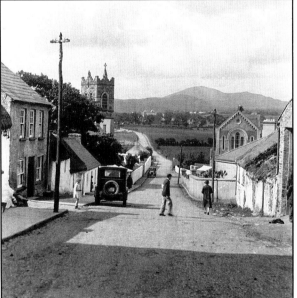

County Derry

St. Eugene's Cathedral is seen reflected in the old city reservoir, 1940. Taken from the end of Westland Terrace, the photograph shows the rear of the houses on Creggan Street, with the Bishop's House on the left. The Cathedral was designed by J. J. McCarthy and built 1851-73.

Panoramic view of Derry's Bogside taken from the scaffolding of the new chapel at St. Columb's College, Bishop Street, 1940. Natives of the Maiden City will recognize the Gasworks in the foreground, the Lone Moor Road in the background and the Gaelic Football pitch left of centre.

A scenic view of Dungiven churchyard in the heart of County Derry. The backdrop is provided by Benbradagh (1535 feet). The photographer was 73 years old when he visited Dungiven in 1953.

The tomb of 'Cooey-na-nGall' at Dungiven Priory, 1953. Cooey-na-nGall, chieftain of the O'Cahan clan, died in 1385.

County Antrim

The village of Waterfoot, near Cushendall, in the winter of 1937. The snow-clad Antrim Plateau drops dramatically into Red Bay where the McDonnells of Scotland landed in days gone by.

At the extreme north-east corner of County Antrim, Torr Head overlooks the Scottish coast. On a clear day, one can even see the houses on the Mull of Kintyre. It was not a clear day when Fr Browne was there in 1937 so he focused on this curious little garden well beside a farmer's cottage.

Belfast

The *Titanic* Memorial in Belfast's city centre (1937), not far from where the ship was built. This must have brought back painful memories for the photographer because he sailed on the first leg of the *Titanic's* maiden voyage, disembarking at Queenstown (Cobh) in 1912. Note the name of the building in the background. The memorial was moved from this site to the eastern side of City Hall in 1970.

Opposite:
Suburban road-works at Dundonald, 1949. Over the roof-tops can be seen the magnificent Government Building, Stormont. This was the seat of the Northern Irish Parliament until it was prorogued in 1972.

'Guarding the School-children' is how Fr Browne captioned this photograph taken on the Falls Road, Belfast in 1949. Traffic wardens, known as Department of Education 'scouts', had just been introduced. Note the trolley-bus, a form of public transport never seen in Dublin.

County Down

Exchanging the latest news at Castle-wellan (1938).

Presbyterian church at Newry (1930) with Georgian Mall in the foreground. The photograph was taken early in the morning of Midsummer's Day.

'Where the Mountains of Mourne sweep
down to the sea' at Newcastle (1934).
Slieve Donard (2,796 feet) can be seen
towering over Dundrum Bay.

'Wafers for little boys; cones for little
girls'. Children enjoy ice-cream at
Rathfriland (1940).

County Armagh

Confirmation Day at Keady, 1933. The
children are pictured in the grounds of
the Catholic church with the Archbishop
of Armagh and Primate of All Ireland,
Cardinal McRory.

Opposite:
'Deserted Village' just north of the new Border (1929). The village of Ball's Mills is on the Glasdrummon — Crossmaglen road. Note the hand-painted sign-post.

Road-bowling on the Armagh-Keady road (1933). This sport is played only in counties Armagh and Cork. Originally practised by soldiers hurling canon-balls, the man here is seen 'throwing the bullet'.

Panoramic view of the ecclesiastical capital of Ireland, Armagh City. The Church of Ireland cathedral is on the sky-line, framed by a doorway of the Roman Catholic cathedral (1934).

County Monaghan

Monaghan railway station (1937). A nostalgic photograph for older Monaghan viewers because the railway was closed in 1957. Note the lanterns and the ornate wrought-iron brackets which support the roof.

A harvest scene near Carrickmacross in 1937. Teams of horses were used in the lakelands of County Monaghan until recent times. Here we see barley stacked in 'stooks' to dry.

Glasslough House, (1949):
Left: The owner, Sir Shane Leslie, in his study. *Below:* Exterior of the house, taken from the north-east.

County Cavan

A view of the fisherman's paradise, Lough Sheelin, in 1934. Although the picture shows geese, it conjures up images of the Children of Lir who, in ancient Celtic mythology, were turned into swans.

Study of an old man at Kilnavart (1939).

This amusing shot was taken in Cavan Town (1938). The photographer entitled it, 'Kid carries kid'.

County Fermanagh

Blacksmiths at work in the forge at Lisnaskea (1930).

Ferry-boat on Upper Lough Erne bears
mixed cargo from Trasna Island (1932).
The ferry was discontinued when Lord
Craigavon opened a new bridge here on
15th April, 1935.

The War Memorial, Enniskillen (1932).
The dates 1939-45 had to be added after
World War II. This was the scene of a
Provisional IRA atrocity in 1987 in which
eleven people died.

County Tyrone

Opposite:
Tranquil scene on the Ulster Blackwater (1934) not far from where the river enters Lough Neagh.

'The Round House' at Omagh (1946). This was the home of the Great Northern Railway locomotives that served on the line between Portadown and Derry which closed in 1957. Note the turntable which directed the engines into their curvilinear shed.

A wee Ulster lass (1939).

LEINSTER

There are many Approved Roads (and even more unapproved ones) between Northern Ireland and the Republic. One of the former is at the village of Blacklion – a very English-sounding name. In fact this is a good example of how some Irish place-names were curiously anglicized. The original Gaelic name for the village was *Bealach Laighean* (pronounced 'bal-ak line'), meaning 'the way to Leinster'.

Each of Leinster's twelve counties was photographed in detail by Fr. Browne. With the arrival of Henry II's forces in the twelfth century, Leinster was the first province to fall under English rule. Over the next few centuries, with many of the invaders becoming 'more Irish than the Irish themselves', the English gradually found themselves confined to 'The Pale': an area stretching from Drogheda at the mouth of the Boyne to Dublin at the mouth of the Liffey. Inland, the Pale was fortified by castles such as those at Trim (the largest Norman ruin in Ireland) and Clongowes Wood (still inhabited; now a Jesuit boarding-school). The latter was formerly called Castle Browne after a family that may well have been among the photographer's ancestors.

The rationale behind the ordering of the counties in this book is that I've taken the maritime ones clockwise around the coast of each province first and then swung inland to present the inland counties in cyclic order. With Leinster, therefore, we begin with County Louth.

In the extreme north of Louth lies the Cooley peninsula. Fr. Browne loved to ramble in its mountains, camera at the ready. No doubt he pondered on the Heroic Age of Cú Chulainn and the heroes of old who performed such superhuman feats as the one described in *Táin Bó Cuailgne* (literally 'the cattle-raid of Cooley'). Not many Dubliners realize that such rugged territory as this can be found an hour and a half from their doorsteps.

It was at Ardee in County Louth that Cú Chulainn died in the lengthy to-hand combat with Ferdia which is commemorated by a fine sculpture by Shepherd in Dublin's General Post Office. Ardee means 'the Ford of Ferdia'. Many another fight took place in County Louth too. In 1318 Edward Bruce, the Scottish King of Ireland was defeated and killed near Dundalk. In 1649 Oliver Cromwell massacred the citizens of Drogheda. And remember the Boyne. It was in 1690 that James II retreated southwards through Louth to be defeated comprehensively by William of Orange at Oldbridge on the border of Meath.

County Meath, in ancient times, formed the nucleus of a fifth province of Ireland based on the seat of the High Kings at Tara. The Province of Meath has, long since, been absorbed into Leinster. Meath has only a few miles of coastline, running south from where the railway crosses the Boyne via an impressive viaduct at Drogheda which Fr. Browne photographed on several occasions and from unusual angles (such as from the footplate of a locomotive).

The reason why Meath reaches to the coast dates to the days when each diocese of Ireland had to have a harbour whence the local bishop could escape overseas. Each diocese still has a 'port of emigration' either on the sea or on the navigable River Shannon.

Travelling south, one has quickly traversed Meath and entered County Dublin. Over 120 photographs from the Browne Collection were published in *The Annals of Dublin: Fair City* (Wolfhound Press, 1987). In this chapter we take the opportunity of presenting some more pictures of the capital.

Dublin was founded by the Vikings in A.D. 841 and remained under foreign control until 1922. Schoolchildren are often told that the High King of Ireland, Brian Boru, expelled the Vikings by his victory at the Battle of Clontarf in 1014. Nothing could be further from the fact that King Sitric, who took no part in that battle, reigned over Dublin before and after that date.

Fr. Browne took over 4,500 photographs of Dublin between 1925 and 1957. One batch of these stands out: the pictures of the Eucharistic Congress in 1932. The other photos of that event, at least the ones which I have seen myself, concentrate on the ceremonies in the Phoenix Park and on O'Connell Bridge. Browne has hundreds of photographs of these, including ones of the V.I.P.'s (such as G. K. Chesterton) who attended, but he has more. He went around the suburbs of the city and showed how places like Drumcondra, Rathfarnham and Donnybrook were decked out for the occasion.

Moving on south to County Wicklow we can soon sense that in such mountainous country we are 'beyond the Pale'. The 'wilde Irishe' of Wicklow, families like the O'Byrnes and the O'Tooles were thorns in the invaders' guts for centuries. In the 19th century, the Military Road – a marvellous piece of engineering often walked by Fr. Browne – was driven right into the heart of Wicklow. It is still driven by tourists when they cross by the Sally Gap on their way to Glendalough.

Monastic ruins and round towers, like those at Glendalough, can be found all over Ireland. Fr. Browne made a habit of photographing these whenever he found himself within reasonable reach of them. He didn't just 'take snaps' like the common or garden sight-seer; he took detailed shots of each architectural feature that would gladden an antiquarian's soul.

County Wicklow is still rich in minerals. In prehistoric times it produced most of the gold of Europe. When Fr. Browne wandered along the mountainy streams above Arklow in 1926, he must have recalled his visit to Ophir Creek

The Custom House, Dublin (1944).

in Australia the previous year where he photographed the remains of the earliest gold-mine on that continent.

Wexford, like Arklow and Wicklow, is a Viking name coming from the Norse root, *Vik*. In 1169 the Normans landed in Ireland at Baginbun in the south of the county. Their method of conquest lay in the construction of castles and Wexford still has more than its fair share of them, e.g. the one at Ballyhack that you will see shortly.

County Kildare is the home of the world-famous Irish bloodstock industry. Fr. Browne loved horses and was even photographed 'astride' as an army chaplain. In Kildare he focused on cavalry manoeuvres on the Curragh, on the old forges that cover the county and on the sundry details of the blacksmith's craft.

Carlow Town has the largest sugar refinery in Ireland. The surrounding countryside has sugar-beet as its main crop. The Browne Collection contains dozens of photographs of this industry in its infancy. Also in County Carlow is Brownshill Dolmen, a majestic megalithic structure. Often called 'Druids' Altars', 'Giants' Tables' or 'Beds of Diarmuid and Gráinne' (two prehistoric lovers), dolmens mark the graves of mighty warriors. The capstone of the one shown here weighs over a hundred tons and is reputed to be the heaviest in Ireland.

Kilkenny, home of the Ormond family that ruled Ireland on and off around the time of the first Queen Elizabeth, boasts of having more medieval buildings, still in use, than any other city in the country. Fr. Browne found it much to his liking. He left us many images of its cathedral, its castles, its narrow and winding streets.

County Laois holds pride of place as the county most photographed by Fr. Browne, the reason being that he lived in Emo for the best part of thirty years (1931-1957). Emo Court, which was built for Lord Portarlington by James Gandon, the architect of Dublin's Custom House and Four Courts, is now open to the public. In Browne's day it was the Jesuit novitiate, its surrounding woods having been taken over by the Forestry Commission. He took, literally, thousands of photographs of forestry skills and took a special interest in the ornithological life of the area. In this, as in other aspects of his work, he liked to specialize. Consequently, we find that he has left us intimate studies of the swan and the tree-creeper. Cygnets hatching and tree-creepers roosting can be seen from all angles.

Bord na Móna, the semi-state body that administers Ireland's turf industry, was founded when Fr. Browne was most prolific. County Offaly was at his doorstep so he was able to record each advance in that fast-expanding industry as it took place. The various peat-burning generating-stations of the Electricity Supply Board he photographed in the course of construction. Since the Jesuits had (and still have) a house near Tullamore, he was able to spend longish periods in Offaly and came to know many of the nomads who lived in little oases in that vast, brown desert.

Mullingar is the County Town of Westmeath and (even though they are not shown here due to lack of space) many photographs in the Collection bear witness to its commerce in the thirties. An entire volume could be produced on *Fair Days in Ireland*. In such a book, Westmeath would figure prominently. The Athlone Town Fair, shown here, is but one of dozens that drew the Browne photographic eye. Athlone is now one of the main 'marinas' for Shannon cruisers. In the Browne era most of the pleasure-craft were powered by oars. One facet of this tourist industry hasn't changed: the old 'watering-holes' where one can quench one's thirst are still in business. He photographed 'The Three Jolly Pigeons' as far back as 1934.

One of the views of County Longford seen in this book shows 'Cobham's Flying Circus'. This is typical of the kind of event that attracted Frank Browne like the proverbial magnet. In the Munster chapter later on you will see the athletic meeting at Ballydavid, County Kerry. Other examples, from elsewhere in the Collection, include Highland Games in Scotland and the sheep-shearing competition at Kangaroobie in the Australian outback.

Overall, these Leinster photographs show us that in Fr. Browne's day, as in our own, there was quite a contrast between urban and rural Ireland. The advent of television, has blurred the distinction to some extent, bringing the carry-on of Dublin and Dallas into the homes of the hinterland. Nevertheless, the people of, say, Kells or Tullamore or villages like Rahan still find it a change to go up to Dublin. They still flock to the Big Town on traditional dates. They still do their Christmas shopping there on 8th December.

County Louth

The road from Ulster to Leinster winds through the Gap of the North. It was used by Cú Chulainn and the Red Branch knights many centuries ago. And remember 1690. Here a cloud of exhaust greets the Free State customs officer at Carrickcarnan in 1930.

The Boyne Viaduct at Drogheda (1925) was built by the Scottish engineer, John McNeill, between 1851 and 1854. The present bridge is a 1932 replacement, built virtually inside of the original structure seen here.

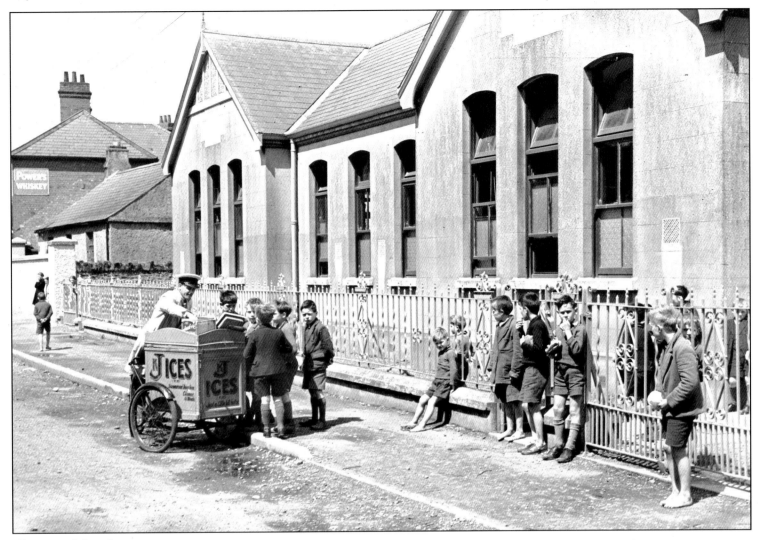

County Meath

The ice-cream man at Dunboyne,
(1937). The picture was taken outside
the National School.

Kells is famous for its Columban monastery from which its eponymous book was stolen in 1007. A fine round tower and several intact Celtic Crosses survive. This incomplete High Cross stands in the Market Place (1928).

Headford House, (1948):
   The staircase, designed by William Adam.
   Lady Headford at her car.
   Miss Elizabeth Clarke pictured with a pedigree Hereford bull.

Dublin City

'The School of Art' is Fr Browne's own caption for this 1939 photograph, taken in Basin Lane.

Children enjoy the fountain in St Stephen's Green (1938).

46

Busy scene at the top of Grafton Street (1939). The Terenure tram is passing 'Smiths of the Green'.

Éamon De Valera, Taoiseach (Prime Minister), at the opening of Kimmage Manor, new seminary for the Holy Ghost Fathers (1938). Here he is being greeted by Bishop Shanahan.

Rathmines Road in 1937. The tower of the Town Hall is on the right with the Technical School and Public Library opposite.

County Dublin

The Bundoran Express at Balbriggan (1946). The railway line to the sea-side resort of Bundoran in County Donegal was closed in 1957.

Enjoying the summer sunshine on Killiney strand in south County Dublin (1925). Donkey-rides continued to provide fun for toddlers until the early 1950s.

County Wicklow

Mr A. O'Leary's car has found the climb
to Glendalough tough going in 1925.

Shelton Abbey, Arklow (1947). The former home of the Earl of Wicklow is now a penitentiary. The house, now bereft of its magnificent furnishings, was built by Sir Richard Morrison, with some help from his son, William Vitruvius, in the 1820s.

County Wexford

The village pump at Ballyhack (1930), with the Norman castle in the background.

The cooper and his children at Kilinnick (1930). The ancient craft of making barrels by hand was carried on as a cottage industry in rural Ireland until the early 1960s.

County Kildare

'Shoeing a wheel' in the olden style at a
forge near Newbridge (1929). On the
right is a cooling tank which was used in
the manufacture of pikes for the 1798
Rebellion.

'Coming':
The local tramp at Two-mile-house,
County Kildare (1938).

'Going'

County Carlow

Swinging on the pump at Leighlinbridge (1940).

The Sullivan children on top of the dolmen (or cromlech) at Brownshill House near Carlow (1942).

County Kilkenny

'Youth and Age' was the photographer's caption for this portrait, taken in County Kilkenny in 1928.

War-time transport in Kilkenny City (1942). The Home and Colonial Stores had branches all over the country at this time. The side-car is of the type still used in Killarney.

County Kilkenny has long been famous for its hurlers. In this 1925 photograph, three youthful enthusiasts discuss a forthcoming clash.

County Laois

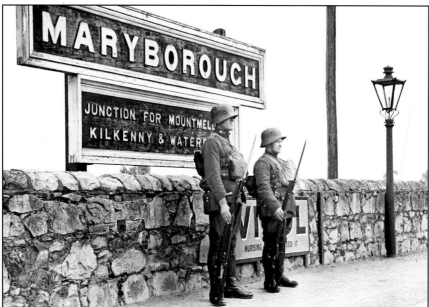

Motor accident on the main Dublin-Cork road at New Inn (1932). The overturned Ford belonged to the County Engineer. Note the 'Baby' Austin in the background.

Attention! Soldiers of the Irish army, wearing German-style helmets, pose for Fr Browne on the platform of Maryborough (now Portlaoise) station in 1940.

There are Holy Wells all over Ireland but none so strange as that of St Fintan at Clonenagh which is half-way up a tree. It is pictured here in 1933.

County Offaly

Harvesting at St Stanislaus' College, Rahan. Here we see the threshing machine in action (1928) and the travelling squad of helpers (the *meitheal*, in Gaelic) at work.

'Eighteen Pence the Lot!', cries the vendor at Tullamore Fair (1929). The long-established premises of Goodbody and Co. can be seen in the background.

Woman and child: a study (1929). Taken at Oughter which was described by Fr Browne as 'a lost city of the Bog'.

County Westmeath

The Church of SS. Peter and Paul, Athlone, in the course of construction (1932). This impressive building, in Roman Renaissance style, with prominent twin spires and graceful dome, overlooks the River Shannon. Note the Guinness building mid-stream: this dates back to the days when kegs of stout were transported by barge.

Athlone Fair (1936). Farmers visit 'The Big Town' for the day to try on the latest fashions in menswear.

Cruising on the River Shannon has become very popular in recent years and many riverside pubs have become well known. 'The Three Jolly Pigeons', seen here in 1934, has been a favourite watering-hole for generations of anglers, locals and patrons from all over the midlands.

County Longford

Fair Day, Longford Town (1940). 'The Emergency', as the Irish called World War II, may be in full swing, but its effects have still to be felt when this picture was taken. The bustling crowd can buy anything from a kneader to an ankle-jack — including a galvanized bucket.

'Cobham's Flying Circus' comes to County Longford (1935). Huge queues formed for free flights. Here we see a parachutist in his bi-plane. Tragically, this man was killed in a parachute jump one week later.

MUNSTER

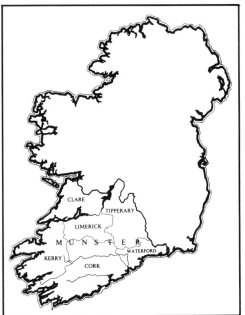

The province of Munster is named after King Mugha who flourished in the second century A.D. and ruled the southern half of Ireland. His northern frontier was the lengthy, ice-age Esker Riada which runs across the midlands; he even 'owned' the half of the city of Dublin south of High Street.

Waterford, outside of Ireland, means glass. Its crystal factory is the largest in the world. On account of its prominence, the glass industry puts Waterford's other industries in the shade. Where would one go to find photographs of the city's other old factories? To the Browne Collection. One example, Cahill & Hearn's Boot Factory, can be seen at the beginning of this chapter.

Waterford (*Vadrefjord*) was founded by the Vikings in A.D. 853 and, because of its proximity to Mainland Europe, it became a key port in the elaborate network of trading links set up by those long-shipped Scandinavians. Reginald's Tower, still in an excellent state of preservation, was built by the local ruler in 1003.

The Norman Conquest which, as we have seen, began in neighbouring County Wexford in 1169, quickly took Waterford into its embrace. The leader of the second wave of Norman invaders was Richard FitzGilbert de Clare, Lord of Strigoil, better known as Strongbow. He captured Waterford in 1170 and it was here that he married Aoife, the eldest daughter of Diarmaid Mac Murrough, King of Leinster.

As with the Vikings, Waterford's Norman rulers found the city ideally sited for trade. It became their second most important port, after Dublin. The port has retained its importance ever since. In recent decades, since Ireland joined the European Community, it has increased its share of the Irish market, especially in the area of beef-exports. With the building of the Channel Tunnel between England and France, a new challenge faces the port of Waterford. It must try to convince Irish exporters that the over-sea route can compete favourably with the under-sea one. Success would appear to lie with the development of specialized container-ships.

Ships of all denominations fascinated Fr. Browne. Queenstown (now Cobh) in Cork Harbour, was the principal British naval base in Ireland when Frank knew it first. His uncle, Robert Browne, was Bishop of Cloyne for many years, and his brother, Fr. William Browne, was the bishop's secretary. Frank usually spent some of his summer holidays in the bishop's house in Queenstown and it was to this address that his ticket for the maiden voyage of *R.M.V. Titanic* was sent in 1912. When the doomed liner was leaving Queenstown, Fr. Browne took the last extant photograph of Captain Smith. As London's *Independent* newspaper put it recently: 'One extraordinarily prophetic shot shows the *Titanic's* captain looking anxiously into one of the ship's lifeboats.'

The Browne Collection contains a large album of shipping prints. Besides the warships of the Royal Navy, it includes the numerous White Star and Cunard liners that used Cobh as a port-of-call. American and German ships are there too, as well as the tenders that served them and the crews who served on the tenders. Steerage-class emigrants are contrasted with first-class globe-trotters and the vital statistics of dozens of liners, such as the ill-fated *Lusitania*, are duly recorded.

Shandon Steeple, Cork (1932).

Cork City is the capital of Munster, and it was here that Frank Browne was born on 3rd January, 1880. His mother, Brigid Mary Browne (née Hegarty) died of puerperal fever eight days later. She was the daughter of James Hegarty J.P. and Ellen Hegarty (née Forde). James Hegarty was a wealthy tanner who owned a lot of property in the Sunday's Well area of the city.

Frank's father, James, was a flour merchant. For most of his married life he lived at Buxton Place, off Sunday's Well Road. The father of eight children, he was drowned while swimming at Crosshaven in County Cork on 2nd September 1989 – a year after Frank had joined the Jesuits.

The photographer-to-be was baptized in the Cathedral of SS. Mary and Anne, Shandon, Cork, on 8th January 1880. He left us photographs of this cathedral and of its Church of Ireland counterpart which is dedicated to Cork's Patron Saint, Finbarr. Cathedrals, indeed, figure prominently in the Collection. The ones at Sydney, Naples and Cologne are but three examples. For *The Kodak Magazine* he photographed the great cathedrals of England in the 1930s. The work he did in Canterbury, York, Norwich, Ely, Winchester and so on has stood the test of time. His articles on the history of these buildings are as informative for the general reader as his details of camera-settings are for the photographic enthusiast.

It is scarcely necessary to say that Fr. Browne took hundreds of photographs of his native city. Since most of these are of a personal nature rather than of public events or of important visitors, they provide a valuable supplement to the huge *Cork Examiner* Collection which is undoubtedly the finest archive of newspaper photographs in Ireland.

County Cork is well represented in the Browne Collection. It is Ireland's largest county, with an area of 2,800 square miles. Frank's brother, William, eventually became Parish Priest of Blarney, so there are lots of pictures of that town and its famous castle. The pejorative word, 'Blarney', is reputed to have originated in the dealings between Queen Elizabeth I and the Lord of Blarney, Cormac Mac Dermott Mac Carthy.

Elizabethan settlers took over most of the Mac Carthy lands and they built castles in most of the picturesque valleys of the county. Kilcolman Castle near Doneraile, for instance, was built by 'the gentle Spenser'. Here he wrote *The Faerie Queen* and a plan for the extermination of the Irish race. Dunboy Castle was the stronghold of the O'Sullivans at Castletownbere. It was the last Irish castle to hold out against Queen Elizabeth's forces before it was finally destroyed in 1602, a year before the Queen's death.

Fr. Browne, as we have seen before, photographed castles both inside and out. On the other hand he loved to visit tranquil spots such as Gougane Barra, the hermitage of Cork's Patron, which is set in magnificent mountain scenery at the source of the River Lee.

Moving on to Kerry we find ourselves – and Fr. Browne – among even higher mountains, the highest in Ireland. Killarney, with its lakes, lies in the midst of these. In the town of Killarney itself, Frank Browne took very fine photographs of the Cathedral of St. Mary, which was designed by Pugin in 1855. A much earlier ecclesiastical building was given similar photographic treatment. Gallarus Oratory, on the Dingle Peninsula, measures just fifteen feet by ten, but it is an excellent example of monastic architecture. Resembling an upturned boat, the oratory has remained completely watertight after more than a thousand years.

The mention of boats recalls the memory of the best-known Kerry saint, Brendan the Navigator (484-577). St. Brendan's House stands at Kilmalkedar on the Dingle Peninsula, and from there to the Saint's Road, an ancient track, supposed to have been built by St. Brendan, winds to the top of Brandon Mountain (3,127 feet). Unlike his clerical predecessor, Fr. Browne climbed this mountain in a distinguished-looking Riley motor-car. His views from the top, including some of the Riley, are quite superb.

From the summit of the Connor Pass he took panoramic photographs, some of which include the distant County Town of Tralee.

From Kerry Head on the estuary of the River Shannon we look across to the south coast of County Clare. The estuary has a deepwater channel for vessels of 200,000 tonnes, and over a hundred square kilometres of shelter. A Dutch firm was commissioned to carry out a survey here in 1982-3. It reported that ships of 400,000 tonnes could be accommodated if dredging operations costing £5 million were undertaken. The estuary, therefore, has a rosy financial future. Already, since Fr. Browne's day, the gigantic alumina plant at Aughinish, and the electrical power-station at Moneypoint have transformed the landscape.

The cliffs of Clare, at over 700 feet, are among the highest in Europe, and many a fabulous Browne picture was taken from the top of them. Clare is also where we find Shannon Airport, known in Frank Browne's time as Rineanna. Obviously he enjoyed photographing old aeroplanes; he took flying lessons himself and took an amusing self-portrait in his pilot's gear. Besides the Shannon Airport photographs, his Collection shows Dublin Airport in the building (when it was called Collinstown) and the military airport at Baldonnell.

One of the County Clare photographs in this book shows a small, rural creamery. The scene, with the donkey-drawn carts, used to be a very familiar one all over the country. Fr. Browne was extremely interested in industrial development, especially in rural Ireland. The dairy industry was still in its early stages of development when he photographed the creameries at work. Every stage in the process of manufacturing large quantities of butter is photographed in its entirety. So detailed, indeed, is one set of these creamery pictures that one has the impression that Fr. Browne was going to give a lecture on the subject to an invited audience. He probably did!

Industrial development on a much larger scale began on the other side of County Clare at Ardnacrusha in 1925. The Shannon hydroelectric scheme took four years to complete, and Browne visited the site several times as construction progressed.

In neighbouring Limerick City he was also a frequent visitor. He used to stay at the Crescent College which was at the top of O'Connell Street at that time. The college has now moved to the suburbs at Dooradoyle, but the Church of the Sacred Heart – the first church in Ireland to be so named – remains where he photographed it.

Fr. Browne frequently stayed at Mungret College, a Jesuit boarding-school in County Limerick, now closed. He photographed the villagers of Mungret and its fifteenth-century church dedicated to St. Nessan, who founded a monastery here in the sixth century.

Nothing remains of Limerick's Viking past, but its Anglo-Norman remains find their place in the Browne Collection. St. Mary's Cathedral (1170) and King John's Castle (1210) are still in admirable condition. I am happy to hear that the extraneous houses which were built in the Castle Yard in the 1930s are finally ear-marked for demolition. Fr. Browne also photographed the Broken Treaty Stone which marks the end of the Siege of Limerick, and its surrender to the army of William of Orange in 1692.

Finally, we come to County Tipperary, heart of the Golden Vale of Ireland, with its rich pastures and the fine dairy herds that provide the raw materials for our most important industry. Because it is such a rich county, Tipperary has many large towns. Thurles, Clonmel, Carrick-on-Suir, Cahir, Cashel, Templemore, Nenagh, Roscrea and Tipperary Town itself all came under Fr. Browne's scrutiny. He also did detailed photographic work at such ecclesiastical sites as Cormac's Chapel on the Rock of Cashel and Holy Cross Abbey.

County Waterford

Small-talk by the water-side (1928). Fr Browne likened this view of Waterford to Bruges in Belgium. The tower of St John's Church can be seen on the sky-line.

This looks like a scene from an American Western (or from the MGM lot in Culver City) but it was actually taken at the seaside resort of Tramore in 1938.

Children 'playing marbles from the knee' in Waterford City (1941).

Lady machinist at work in Cahill & Hearn's Boot Factory, Waterford (1941).

Cork City

Dockers waiting for work on the quays (1933). Still a busy international port, this picture shows the German merchantman *Elbe* about to be unloaded.

Fishermen at work on the River Lee near Blackrock (1930). As in the estuaries of other rivers, the salmon net was dropped in a semi-circle by rowing-boat.

This poster outside a city theatre took Fr Browne's fancy in 1938. Obviously, he was amused to see what would follow the Men's Mission which he preached in March of that year.

The City Hall being built (1932) of limestone from the nearby Little Island quarries. Opened in 1936, its Assembly Hall can seat 2,000 people.

Cobh

The consecration of St Colman's Cathedral, Queenstown (now Cobh) on 12th August, 1919. The ceremony coincided with the silver episcopal jubilee of the photographer's uncle, Bishop Robert Browne of Cloyne. Designed by E. W. Pugin, G. C. Ashlin and T. A. Coleman, the building of St Colman's had started in 1896.

Mackerel-fishing at Deepwater Quay (1941). Some of the people in this photograph can be recognized by inhabitants of Cobh today.

The Cunard Wharf (1930). The 300-feet high spire of St Colman's Cathedral gave a last glimpse of Ireland to many departing emigrants. Scott's Shipping Agents, who issued Fr Browne's *Titanic* ticket in 1912, are still in business here.

Sailors at work in the rigging of the *C. B. Peterson*, from Australia (1930).

County Cork

Panoramic view of Bantry (1931) taken from scaffolding on the tower of the Church of Ireland. Whiddy Island, destined to become an oil terminal, can be seen in the middle of Bantry Bay.

Haytime at Allihies (1936). The haven of Castletownbere can be seen in the distance.

The Booth family have a picnic at Mizen Head (1930). Notice how the back seat of the motor-cars of those days could be removed to make an outdoor couch.

Main Street, Mitchelstown (1938). The driver of an old Ford Prefect is finding it hard to get through.

County Kerry

At the Eagle's Nest, Killarney (1926).
The Bourke family from Dublin are
taking a motoring holiday through
Ireland's highest mountains.

A poignant scene at Brandon Cove
(1932). The newly-tarred currachs have
been put up here to dry.

Sports Day at Ballydavid (Baile na nGall) in 1932. Note the old method of doing the high jump. The spectators here are native speakers of Gaelic.

County Clare

Shannon Airport, Rineanna (1946).
Above: The Control Tower, interior.
Below: Passengers boarding a Pan American Airways 'Constellation'.

The Horse Fair at Kilrush (1939). The intense discussions seen here explain how the expression 'horse trading' came to be coined.

Donkeys and carts queue up outside the Cooraclare Creamery (1944). Scenes like this are still commonplace in some parts of rural Ireland.

A 'donkey team' on the road near Scarriff (1944): a highly unusual form of transportation, even in war-time.

The West Clare Railway: taking on water
at Ennis station (1944). This narrow-
gauge railway was immortalized in Percy
French's song, 'Are you right there,
Michael?'

County Limerick

The 'Shanachie', a traditional Irish story-teller, at Carrigogunnell (1925).

Limerick Docks (1936). Note the sea gates — and how little traffic is passing along Dock Road at the time shown on the clock-tower.

'Beauty and the Beast': the macabre
dance of girl with goat at Kildimo (1939).

County Tipperary

The stone roof of Cormac's Chapel on the Rock of Cashel was built in 1127 and photographed here in 1926. The picture was taken from the top of the adjacent Round Tower.

Main Street, Roscrea (1930). On the left is Ormonde Castle, built in the thirteenth century. The gables and chimneys seen here were added in the seventeenth century.

The 'Car Park', Cahir (1942). The shortage of petrol explains the absence of cars.

The West Gate, Clonmel (1932).
Originally part of the medieval wall of
the town, this gate was rebuilt in its
present form in 1831.

CONNACHT

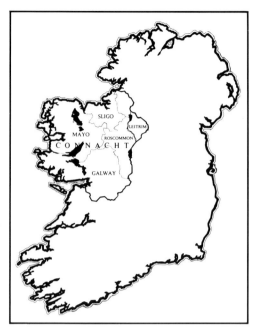

'To Hell or to Connacht!', said Cromwell to the Irish in 1649, condemning them to that province of stone and stone walls, west of the Shannon. Hell it might be to the farmer, but Connacht is a photographer's paradise. Fr. Browne's work often brought him to each of the five counties. He also sailed to Aran on several occasions and took hundreds of photographs on all of those islands.

Galway, the capital of Connacht, has grown in stature during the 20th century. In the early 1900s it became a university city and in the past decade it has become one of the fastest-growing urban areas in Ireland. The origins of the town are uncertain, but it is believed to be the 'Magnata' mentioned by the Alexandrian geography, Ptolemy, in A.D. 130 *The Annals of the Four Masters* state that the Connachtman built a fort here in 1124. The Anglo-Norman knight, Richard de Burgh (an ancestor of Chris, the singer) captured the city and made it his residence. Among its settlers were the families who later became known as 'the fourteen tribes of Galway'. We know the names of these fourteen families: two of them were the Brownes and the Joyces. It is interesting to note that the fathers of both Frank Browne and James Joyce were born in Cork but had Galway connections. Both Frank and James attended the same school in Dublin, Belvedere College, and they studied the same courses in the same years at the Royal University (1899-1902). I have yet to discover whether Frank ever photographed his famous literary contemporary.

The Jesuit church in Galway is situated near the 'Egg Market', shown in this chapter. Whenever Fr. Browne was staying with his confrères there, he would make a habit of lingering near the market with his camera and would snap buyers and sellers when they were least suspecting. For centuries Galway traded extensively with Spain. It thus acquired distinctive Spanish features which can still be seen in the Claddagh area, notably in the dress and manners of the people. An example, dated 1925, is shown here.

The Corrib is better known for its sailing and trout but, curiously, Fr. Browne seems to have been more intrigued by its eel fisheries – judging by the number of photographs he took of the eel-nets being raised in Galway, sometimes by a well-dressed gentleman in a polka-dot bow-tie.

County Galway includes the great, mountainous expanse of Connemara, now sparsely peopled, but formerly a 'congested district' before the Great

Famine of the 1840s reduced Ireland's population from eight million to five. Emigration still takes its toll here: witness the closure of the railways. We have already seen a picture of the old West Clare railway, now defunct. In Fr. Browne's time there was also a line through Connemara from Galway to Clifden. He took a wide-lens self-portrait showing the railway-station at Maam with the Twelve Bens in the background.

As an aside, I might mention that there are about twenty self-portraits in the Collection. Two that took my fancy were entitled 'Me and the Elephant' (1924) and 'Self in Rickshaw, Kandy, Ceylon' (1925). Also, we have about a dozen photographs of Frank Browne taken by others. The first of these was taken by the firm of Francis Guy in Cork when Frank was aged four (1884). Another was taken by Fr. (later Monsignor) Joseph Scannell among the ruins of Arras, France, after the bombardment of 1918.

An enthralling documentary film could be made from the Browne photographs of the Aran Islands. He took well over seven hundred pictures there, showing a way of life that has changed very little over the decades. Families sitting quietly by their open hearth (e.g. the Flaherty's of Oghil, 1938) are contrasted with fishermen plying their canvas currachs in a wave-tossed Atlantic; happy groups of wedding-parties are juxtaposed with the half-famished faces of survivors being taken ashore by dauntless lifeboatmen. Pre-historic forts, monastic ruins, holy wells, cliffs, shawls and sweaters: Browne has photographed them.

Nowadays you can fly to Aran and you can fly to Knock in County Mayo. Fr. Browne made several pilgrimages to the shrine of Our Lady at Knock, travelling both by train and car. His priestly work entailed retreat-giving to convents of nuns and he made a practice of photographing these convents for the record. Nuns were responsible for establishing the Providence Woollen Mills at Foxford in County Mayo, that gave such badly-needed employment in the area. Fr. Browne shows us where blankets were manufactured, and shows us the 'cottage industries' of this county from Belmullet to Ballinrobe. Castlebar, the County Town, can be seen too, as can Ballina, Ballintubber, Westport and Newport.

The Cross of Cong, County Mayo, is one of Ireland's most famous master-pieces of religious art. It can be seen in the National Museum in Dublin, where Fr. Browne photographed it along with our other Celtic treasures, such as the Ardagh Chalice and the Tara Brooch.

County Sligo is the Yeats Country. William Butler Yeats spent many summer holidays with his relations here, and his early poems in particular are full of the magical place-names of this county: Lissadel, Knocknarea, Innisfree, to mention just three. While Yeats was writing about them, Browne was photographing them. Interestingly, like Yeats, he was taken by the beauty of Drumcliffe churchyard and took pictures of it long before the poet decided he would like to be buried there.

Dún Aengus, Aran (1938).

When you visit the graveyard to-day, you see Yeats' tombstone with its philosophical epitaph:

Cast a cold Eye
On Life, on Death
Horseman, pass by!

Yeats died in France in 1939 and was originally buried at Roquebrune. He was re-interred at Drumcliffe in 1948. Just recently, I came across an interesting explanation of the enigmatic inscription on his grave. It appears that in Celtic mythology Ben Bulben, a mountain in the north of County Sligo, was the final resting-place of those gallant horsemen, the Fianna. After sundown, they still come riding down the mountain on their way to visit Queen Maeve, who lies under a sepulchral cairn on the top of Knocknarea in the south of the county. It was to these ghostly riders (as well as to you and me and the American students who attend the Yeats' Summer School annually) that the poet was referring.

The Leitrim County Librarian has already taken the initiative of acquiring a selection of Fr. Browne's Leitrim photographs for the benefit of his customers. When the Collection has been saved (i.e. when the Browne negatives have been transferred from dangerous and deteriorating nitrate-based stock to safety film), my hope is that other County Librarians will follow suit.

Fr. Browne's Leitrim photographs feature Ireland's largest coal-mine at Arigna and the monastery at Fenagh (said to have been founded by St. Columba), which became famous as a divinity school under the presidency of St. Killian.

The inhabitants of County Leitrim will be the first to agree that theirs is a poverty-stricken county, badly hit by emigration. An example of its poverty was photographed by Fr. Browne and is shown in this chapter. As a priest, of course, he was distressed by such poverty and must have wondered what he could do about it. I believe that the pictures he took of creameries and cottage industries were shown on screen wherever he thought that a lesson might be learnt. We do know that he travelled around the country with a projector and lantern-slides.

Ireland's 'travelling people', in his day called 'tinkers', were photographed all over the country, particularly in the west. Many of these pictures were reproduced a few years ago in a book by Mr. & Mrs. Gmelch which was published by the O'Brien Press, Dublin.

Finally, we come to County Roscommon. We have seen already that Fr. Browne gave extensive camera coverage to the Celtic monasteries of Ireland. Similarly, he put together a comprehensive record of our Cistercian monasteries, ancient and modern. He made prints of the best of these photographs and filled two albums entitled 'The Cistercian Abbeys of Ireland'.

Boyle, in County Roscommon, was one of the most important sites of the Cistercian monks. Fr. Browne took careful photos of its Norman architectural details. The Cistercians had been introduced into Ireland by the Anglo-Norman conquerors, and the monks themselves came from England and Wales. 'No Irish need apply' was the order of those days. Browne's studies of Boyle, and of the abbeys at Jerpoint, Mellifont, Graiguenamanagh etc., demonstrate the expertise of the architects of old. His pictures of the abbeys that are still flourishing show how the Irish Cistercians of the 20th century are maintaining the traditions established by their predecessors a long time ago.

In County Roscommon, Fr. Browne also photographed the 19th century manor-house at Clonalis, now open to the public. The present owner, Pyers O'Conor-Nash, belongs to the twenty-fifth generation in direct descent from the last High King of Ireland, Rory O'Conor, who abdicated after the Anglo-Norman invasion of 1169 – which makes the O'Conors the oldest royal line in Europe.

Fr. Browne visited Clonalis as a guest of the last O'Conor Don, Fr. Charles O'Conor S.J., a confrère of his in the Jesuit Order, who went on to become its Irish Provincial Superior. It was this Fr. O'Conor, an uncle of Pyers, who celebrated the first Mass in the restored Ballintubber Abbey, County Mayo in 1960s. This Augustinian abbey had been founded by his ancestor, Cathal O'Conor, King of Connacht, in 1216. One of the boasts of the abbey is that Mass has continued to be said there throughout the 774 years of its existence.

Before finishing, let me add a few words on Browne the photographer. Since his career with the camera spanned sixty years (1897-1957), it is understandable that his technique improved as time went by. His work in the 1950s shows a professional touch when compared with his output from the 1920s. We must remember, of course, that the technology of photography improved enormously during his life-time. Cameras and films became more and more sensitive, less and less cumbersome. A glance at Fr. Browne's insurance-policy, still extant, shows that he was able to keep pace with developments. He changed from a Contax I to a Contax II in the early 1930s and ended up with a Leica. His early work shows how lengthy time-exposures were necessary and how easily these could be marred by some obtrusive movement. When 35mm film was invented, Browne's 35mm camera was one of the first of its kind in Ireland.

Because he captioned and dated his photographs so painstakingly, it is clear that Fr. Browne hoped that some day they would be worth publishing. I would like to thank Seamus Cashman of Wolfhound Press, for turning Browne's hope into reality, and David Davison for making the prints.

Fr. Browne took over 42,000 photographs during his life-time. It's hardly surprising to hear that one of these shows the Jesuit burial-plot in Glasnevin Cemetery, Dublin, the spot where he now rests in peace.

County Galway

'Seven so far': this family portrait was taken in Ballinasloe (1938). Notice that the trough outside the cottage window has been converted into a seat.

At the Galway Egg Market (1939). Hens, ducks and general merchandise could be purchased as well as eggs.

Claddagh Fashions (1925). The Claddagh is said to be the oldest fishing village in Ireland. Its inhabitants still form a distinct community within the city of Galway.

The Corrib is better known for its salmon and trout but what we see here is the Corrib Eel Fisheries in Galway City (1932).

The interior of Mrs Kavanagh's cottage at Annaghdown (1942).

At the weighbridge, Oughterard (1925).

The Aran Islands

Girls perched on the 300-feet high perpendicular cliffs at Inishmore watch fishermen ply their curragh through the Atlantic swell (1938).

Dubhchathair, two miles west of Killeany, may be the oldest of the prehistoric forts on the Aran Islands (1925).

The Aran Islands

Man of Aran: portrait of 'Old Tom' Conneely of Cowragh (1938).

At the Aran Life Boat Station on Tuesday 15th August, 1938. Earlier in the day these men had brought back survivors from the wreck of the S.S. *Nogi*.

Fisherman on horseback (1925) near the port of Kilronan which can be seen in the background.

County Mayo

Passengers at Manulla Junction, County Mayo (1941).

The thatcher bringing home his raw materials at Burrishoole, near Newport (1939).

Manufacturers display their wares at the factory of Erris Toys Ltd., Belmullet (1938).

Children at Keel, Achill Island (1939). Dooagh Head can be seen across the bay. The notice-board (centre) warns bathers to beware of porbeagle sharks.

Fishing for salmon on the River Moy at Ballina (1932). In the background is St Muredach's College.

'Oyez! Oyez'! The Town Crier, Foxford, County Mayo (1938). The latest news was delivered like this until recent years in some rural parts of the country.

County Sligo

Magheraghanrush Court Cairn at Deerpark (1929). The prehistoric remains here, including a central court fifty feet long, are among the finest of their kind in Ireland.

Opposite:
Card sharks on Lough Gill (1933). The proceedings of the clergy are being monitored by Canon O'Beirne.

The Crossing: Bringing home the cattle (1933). Local farmers used – and still use – Church Island in Lough Gill for grazing purposes.

Sligo Abbey (1933). Despite its name, this is actually a Dominican priory dating back to 1252. What we see here is the 1414 building, constructed after the original monastery had been destroyed by a fire caused by a candle.

County Leitrim

Scene in an isolated cottage near Cloone
where home spinning was still done in
1933.

A canvas home in the Leitrim hills near Mohill (1933).

Portrait of a coal miner at the Arigna Mine in County Leitrim (1933).

The Arigna Coal Mine (1933). At one of Ireland's few coal deposits, fairly primitive methods of open mining were used at this time. Lough Allen can be seen in the distance.

The tailor's cottage, near Cloone (1933).
Mr Milton hardly posed a threat to Savile
Row!

County Roscommon

Rockingham House, Lough Key (1948).
The house was destroyed by fire in 1957
and is now demolished.
Left: The Grand Staircase.
Below: Rear of House.
Bottom left: Dining Room.
Bottom right: The Great Hall.

Hope and Prudence French, daughters of Lord de Freyne, in the grounds of their home at Frenchpark (1934).

'The Shadow of Progress' is how
Fr Browne describes this reflection
on a thatched house in Keadue (1935).